NINJA FOOD
SMART XL GRILL
COOKBOOK
FOR BEGINNERS

Effortless Delicious and Healthy Recipes to Fry, Bake, Grill and Roast for Your Smart XL Grill

By
Michelle Lively

Disclaimer

Please note, the information written in this book, are for educational and entertainment purposes only. Strenuous efforts have been made to provide accurate, up to date and reliable complete information in this book. All recommendations are made without guarantee on the part of the author and publisher. By reading this document, the reader agrees that under no circumstances are we responsible for any losses, direct or indirect, which are incurred as a result of the use of the information contained in this document, including but not limited to errors, omissions or inaccuracies.

•••

Table of Contents

INTRODUCTION

Are you looking for delicious and effortless recipes to take advantage of the amazing versatility of your Ninja Foodi Smart XL Grill?

If this is what you are looking for then keep reading...

The Ninja Foodi Smart XL Grill delivers your perfect doneness without the guesswork.

In addition, as you know, this amazing appliance is the perfect companion in the kitchen, both for large families, for anyone who wants to grill indoor without losing the outdoor grill taste, and for anyone who want to air fry for eat crispy and crunchy food with guilt-free.

The Ninja Foodi Smart XL Grill is the Smart XL grill that sears, sizzles, and air fry crisps. It possesses an XL capacity and innovative Smart Cook System, grill even more and reaches your desired doneness with the touch of a button. It's also an air fry crisper so you can enjoy your favorite guilt-free fried foods.

Perfectly cook food on the inside to your desired doneness and char grill every side with 500F Cyclonic Grilling Technology and the Smart Cook System. 500F cyclonic air and the 500F grill grate combine to give you delicious char-grilled marks and flavors. It has a Smart Cook System—4 smart protein settings, 9 customizable doneness levels, and the Foodi Smart Thermometer enable you to achieve the perfect doneness with the touch of a button. They can be used to grill 50% more food than the original Ninja Foodi Grill for delicious family sized meals. It is versatile and grills your favorite foods to char grilled perfection, or go beyond grilling with 5 additional cooking functions: Air Crisp, Bake, Roast, Broil, and Dehydrate

What is Ninja Foodi Smart XL Grill

As the name suggests, Ninja Foodi Smart XL Grill can be used to air crisp, bake, roast, broil and dehydrate your favorite food with the touch of a button. It air fry crisps with up to 75% less fat than deep frying using the crisper basket. The versatility of the grill, saying the "air crisp function allows you to emulate deep frying without the large amount of oil.

The grill function by type of meat is awesome especially with the thermometer. It allows you to select how cooked you want your meat and have no smoke. It's the perfect time to grab this multitasking wonder.

Getting to Know the Ninja Foodi Smart XL Grill

Function Buttons:

GRILL: Grill indoors while creating even char, grill marks, and grilled flavor.

AIR CRISP: For crispiness and crunch with little to no oil.

BAKE: Bake cakes, treats, desserts, and more.

ROAST: Tenderize meats, roast vegetables, and more.

DEHYDRATE: Dehydrate meats, fruits, and vegetables for healthy snacks.

BROIL: Add the crispy finishing touch to meals or melt cheese on sandwiches.

Operating Buttons:

POWER button: The power button can be used to turn on the unit once the unit is plugged in. Pressing it during cooking stops the current cooking function and turns off the unit.

Left arrows: Use the up and down arrows to the left of the display to adjust the cooking temperature in any function or to set the internal doneness when using PRESET and MANUAL buttons.

Right arrows: Use the up and down arrows to the right of the display to set the food type when using PRESET or to adjust the cook time when not cooking with the Foodi Smart Thermometer.

MANUAL button: This button can be used to switch the display screen to manually set the thermometer internal doneness. Manual button does not work with Dehydrate function.

PRESET button: Switches the display screen so you can set the thermometer, food type, and internal doneness based on the preset temperatures. Preset button does not work with Dehydrate function. Press the up and down arrows to adjust the temperature or time during cooking. The unit will then resume at those settings.

START/STOP button: After selecting temperature and time, press the START/STOP button to start cooking.

Standby Mode: The unit usually goes into standby mode when there's no interaction with the control panel for 10 minutes and the unit is not cooking.

Preheat: Once the unit is preheating, it will be observed by a progress bar on the display screen and the PREHEAT button will illuminate. To turn off Preheat, press the PREHEAT button while the grill is in preheat state. ADD FOOD will display

Cleaning Your Ninja Foodi Smart XL Grill

❖ The unit should be cleaned thoroughly after every use. Always let the appliance cool before cleaning.

❖ Unplug the unit from the wall outlet before cleaning. Leave the hood open after transfer your food to a serving bowl to let the unit cool quicker.

❖ The cooking pot, grill grate, crisper basket, splatter shield, cleaning brush, and any other included accessories are dishwasher safe, except the thermometer. DO NOT place the thermometer in the dishwasher.

❖ For the best dishwasher cleaning results, you have to rinse the grill grate, crisper basket, splatter shield, and any other accessories with warm water before placing them in the dishwasher.

❖ If hand-washing, you can use cleaning brush to wash the parts. Use the opposite end of the cleaning brush to scrap off any browned bits that's stuck to the unit. Air-dry or pat dry with a paper towel after hand-washing. DO NOT use liquid cleaning solution on or near the thermometer jack. Use a compressed air or a cotton swab to avoid damaging the jack.

❖ When any food residue or grease are stuck on the grill grate, splatter shield, or any other removable part, soak in warm soapy water before cleaning.

❖ Clean the splatter shield after every use. Soaking the splatter shield for a couple of minutes or hours can help soften the baked-on grease.

❖ After soaking, use the cleaning brush to remove the grease from the stainless-steel frame and front tabs.

❖ Deep clean the splatter shield by placing it in a pot of water and boiling it for about 10 minutes to soften the residue or grease. Rinse with room temperature water and allow to dry completely.

❖ To deep clean the thermometer, soak the stainless-steel tip and silicone grip in warm, soapy water. DO NOT immerse the cord or jack in water or any other liquid.

❖ The Foodi Smart Thermometer holder is handwash only. DO NOT use abrasive tools or cleaners. NEVER immerse the main unit in water or any other liquid.

Troubleshooting Tips

"Add Food" appears on the control panel display.

The unit has preheated already and its time to add the ingredients to be cooked.

"Shut Lid" appears on the control panel display.

The hood is open and needs to be closed for the selected function to start.

"Plug In" appears on the control panel display.

It means that the thermometer is not plugged into the jack on the right side of the control panel. Plug the thermometer in before proceeding. Press the thermometer in until you hear a click.

"PRBE ERR" appears on the control panel display.

This happens when the unit timed out before food reached the set internal temperature. As a protection for the unit, it can run for only certain lengths of time at specific temperatures.

"E" appears on the control panel display.

The unit is not functioning properly. You can Contact Customer Service for further assistance.

Why is my food overcooked or undercooked even though I used the thermometer?

It is vital to insert the thermometer lengthwise into the thickest part of the ingredient to get the most accurate reading.

Why does the preheat progress bar not start from the beginning?

When the unit is warm from previously being used, it will not require the full preheating time.

Can I cancel or override preheating?

Preheating is highly recommended for accurate results, but you can omit it by selecting the PREHEAT button after you press the START/STOP button.

Should I add my ingredients before or after preheating?

Allow the unit to preheat before adding your ingredients.

Why is my unit emitting smoke?

When using the Grill function, always select the recommended temperature setting.

How do I pause the unit so I can check my food?

When the hood is opened during a cooking function, the unit will automatically pause.

Will the thermometer grip melt if it touches the hot grill grate?

No, the grip is made of a high-temperature silicone that can handle the Ninja Foodi Smart XL Grill's high temperatures.

My food is burned.

Never add your ingredients until recommended preheat time is complete. Always check the progress throughout cooking, and remove food when desired level of brownness has reached. Transfer the food to serving bowl immediately after the cook time is complete to avoid overcooking.

Why did a circuit breaker trip while using the unit?

The unit uses 1760 watts of power, so it is absolutely important to be plugged into an outlet on a 15-amp circuit breaker. An outlet of 10-amp breaker will lead to the breaker to trip. The unit should be the only appliance plugged into an outlet when in use.

Why does the unit have a 1–9 scale for the Beef Preset?

The 1–9 scale provides a wide range of options for each doneness level so you can customize doneness to your liking.

BREAKFAST RECIPES

Breakfast Frittata

Preparation time: 10 minutes

Cooking Time: 10 minutes

Overall time: 20 minutes

Serves: 3 people

Recipe Ingredients:

- ❖ ½ cup of parmesan cheese
- ❖ 6 grated and divided cherry tomatoes
- ❖ 1 halved bacon slice
- ❖ 3 chopped eggs
- ❖ Salt and black pepper
- ❖ 6 sliced fresh mushrooms
- ❖ 1 tablespoon of olive oil

Cooking Instructions:

1. Select the "Grill" button on the Ninja Foodi Smart XL Grill and regulate the time for 10 minutes at Medium.

2. In a bowl, mix mushrooms, bacon, tomatoes, salt, and black pepper. After that, whisk eggs with cheese in another bowl.

3. Place the bacon mixture in the Ninja Foodi when it shows **"Add Food"** and top it with egg mixture.

4. Grill for about 10 minutes, flipping halfway through cooking. Once done, plate, serve and enjoy.

Bacon Bombs

Preparation time: 5 minutes

Cooking Time: 7 minutes

Overall time: 12 minutes

Serves: 4 people

Recipe Ingredients:

- ❖ 3 large lightly beaten eggs
- ❖ 4 ounces of whole-wheat pizza dough
- ❖ 3 bacon slices of freshly prepared Cooking spray
- ❖ 1 ounce of crisped and crumbled softened cream cheese
- ❖ 1 tablespoon fresh chives, chopped

Cooking Instructions:

1. Firstly, select the "Bake" button on the Ninja Foodi Smart XL Grill and regulate the time for 16 minutes at 350°F.

2. Crack eggs in a non-stick pan and stir, then fry for 1 minute. Stir in the bacon, chives, and cream cheese and keep aside.

3. Cut the pizza dough into 4 equal pieces and roll each into circles.

4. Put ¼ of the bacon-egg mixture in the center of the dough circle and seal the edges with water.

5. Place the doughs in the Ninja Foodi when it shows **"Add Food"** and spray them with cooking oil.

6. Bake for 6 minutes and dish out to serve warm. Enjoy!

Breakfast Pockets

Preparation time: 5 minutes

Cooking Time: 11 minutes

Overall time: 16 minutes

Serves: 3 to 6 people

Recipe Ingredients:

- ❖ 1 box puff pastry sheets (5 eggs)

- ❖ ½ cup of cooked sausage crumbles

- ❖ ½ cup of cooked bacon

- ❖ ½ cup of shredded cheddar cheese

Cooking Instructions:

1. Select the "Bake" button on the Ninja Foodi Smart XL Grill and regulate the time for 10 minutes at 370°F.

2. Crack eggs in a non-stick pan and stir thoroughly then fry for 1 minute. After that, stir in the bacon and sausages and keep aside.

3. Cut the puff pastry into equal-sized rectangles and add a scoop of egg mixture and cheese in the center.

4. Seal the edges with water and transfer into the Ninja Foodi when it shows ***"Add Food."***

5. Spray them with cooking oil and bake for 10 minutes.

6. Dish out in a platter and serve warm.

Avocado Flautas

Preparation time: 10 minutes

Cooking Time: 15 minutes

Overall time: 25 minutes

Serves: 4 to 8 people

Recipe Ingredients:

- ❖ 8 lightly beaten eggs
- ❖ 1 tablespoon of butter
- ❖ ½ teaspoon of salt
- ❖ 1½ teaspoons of cumin
- ❖ 8 fajita size tortillas
- ❖ 8 slices of cooked bacon
- ❖ ½ cup of crumbled feta cheese
- ❖ ¼ teaspoon of pepper
- ❖ 1 teaspoon of chili powder
- ❖ 4 ounces of softened cream cheese
- ❖ ½ cup of mexican shredded avocado crème cheese,
- ❖ ½ cup of sour cream
- ❖ ½ teaspoon of salt
- ❖ 2 small avocados
- ❖ 1 lime juiced
- ❖ ¼ teaspoon of black pepper

Cooking Instructions:

1. Select the **"Air Crisp"** button on the Ninja Foodi Smart XL Grill and regulate the time for 10 minutes at 400°F.

2. Put butter in a skillet on medium heat and add eggs. Stir-fry for 3 minutes and add salt, chili powder, pepper, and cumin.

3. Spread cream cheese on the tortillas and place bacon pieces over them. Top with egg mixture and shredded cheese.

4. Tightly roll each tortilla and place them in the Ninja Foodi when it shows **"Add Food".** Then Air crisp for 12 minutes, flipping halfway through.

5. Put the avocado crème ingredients in a blender and process until smooth.

6. Dish out the baked flautas in a platter and serve warm with avocado cheese and cotija cheese. Delicious!

Sausage and Cheese Wraps

Preparation time: 5 minutes

Cooking Time: 8 minutes

Overall time: 13 minutes

Serves: 4 people

Recipe Ingredients:

❖ 2 pieces of American cheese, (cut into quarters Ketchup, for dipping)

❖ 8 heat and serve sausages

❖ 1 can of 8 counts refrigerated crescent roll dough,

Cooking Instructions:

1. Select the "Grill" button on the Ninja Foodi Smart XL Grill and regulate the time for 10 minutes at Medium.

2. Put the sausage and cheese on each crescent roll. Then wrap the sausages inside the rolls and seal the ends.

3. Place the rolls in the Ninja Foodi when it shows **"Add Food"**. Grill for 8 minutes, flipping halfway through cooking.

4. Serve warm and enjoy.

Swiss Cheese Sandwiches

Preparation time: 5 minutes

Cooking Time: 18 minutes

Overall time: 23 minutes

Serves: 2 people

Recipe Ingredients:

- ❖ 3 tablespoons of half and half cream
- ❖ 2 slices sourdough, white or multigrain bread
- ❖ 1 egg
- ❖ ¼ teaspoon of vanilla extract
- ❖ 2½ ounces of swiss cheese, sliced
- ❖ 2 ounces of deli turkey sliced powdered sugar
- ❖ 2 ounces sliced deli ham,
- ❖ 1 teaspoon butter, melted raspberry jam, for serving

Cooking Instructions:

1. Select the "Grill" button on the Ninja Foodi Smart XL Grill and regulate the time for 18 minutes at Medium.

2. Mix egg with vanilla extract and a half and half cream in a bowl. Then top each bread slice with turkey, ham, and Swiss cheese slice.

3. Cover with the remaining bread slices and press tightly. Then dip in the egg mixture and place them in the Ninja Foodi when it shows **"Add Food".**

4. Grill for 18 minutes, flipping halfway through. Dish out and top with raspberry jam and powdered sugar to serve.

5. Enjoy!

Cajun Sausages

Preparation time: 5 minutes

Cooking Time: 20 minutes

Overall time: 25 minutes

Serves: 3 people

Recipe Ingredients:

- ❖ 1 teaspoon of chili flakes
- ❖ 1½ pounds of ground sausage
- ❖ 1 teaspoon of dried thyme
- ❖ ½ teaspoon of paprika
- ❖ ½ teaspoon of cayenne
- ❖ 2 teaspoons of brown sugar
- ❖ 2 teaspoons of tabasco
- ❖ 1 teaspoon of onion powder
- ❖ Sea salt and black pepper,
- ❖ 3 teaspoons of minced garlic

Cooking Instructions:

1. Start by pressing the "Grill" button on the Ninja Foodi Smart XL Grill and regulate the time for 20 minutes at medium.

2. Combine ground sausage with Tabasco sauce, spices, and herbs in a bowl. Make sausages-shaped patties out of this mixture.

3. Place the patties in the Ninja Foodi when it shows **"Add Food."** Grill for 20 minutes, flipping halfway through cooking.

4. Dish out in a platter and serve warm. Yummy!

CHICKEN RECIPES

Southern-Style Chicken

Preparation time: 5 minutes

Cooking Time: 20 minutes

Overall time: 25 minutes

Serves: 3 to 6 people

Recipe Ingredients:

- ❖ 1 tablespoon of fresh minced parsley
- ❖ 2 cups of crushed Ritz crackers
- ❖ 1 teaspoon of garlic salt
- ❖ ½ teaspoon of black pepper
- ❖ ¼ teaspoon of rubbed sage
- ❖ 1 (3 to 4 pounds) of broiler/fryer chicken (cut up)
- ❖ 1 teaspoon of paprika
- ❖ ¼ teaspoon of ground cumin
- ❖ 1 large beaten egg,

Cooking Instructions:

1. Select the "Air Crisp" button on the Ninja Foodi Smart XL Grill and regulate the time for 20 minutes at 350ºF.

2. Whisk egg in a bowl and combine the rest of the ingredients except for chicken in another bowl.

3. Dip the chicken in the whisked egg and then dredge in the crackers mixture.

4. Place the chicken in the Ninja Foodi when it shows **"Add Food."** Air crisp for about 20 minutes.

5. Dish out immediately and serve warm. Enjoy!

Sesame Chicken Breast

Preparation time: 5 minutes

Cooking Time: 20 minutes

Overall time: 25 minutes

Serves: 2 people

Recipe Ingredients:

- ❖ 2 tablespoons of sesame oil
- ❖ 2 chicken breasts
- ❖ 1 teaspoon of kosher salt
- ❖ ½ teaspoon of black pepper
- ❖ ¼ teaspoon of cayenne pepper
- ❖ 1 tablespoon of onions powder
- ❖ 1 tablespoon of sweet paprika
- ❖ 1 tablespoon of garlic powder

Cooking Instructions:

1. Start by pressing the "Bake" button on the Ninja Foodi Smart XL Grill and adjust the time for 20 minutes at 380ºF.

2. Season the chicken breasts with sesame oil and all other spices. Place the chicken in the Ninja Foodi when it shows **"Add Food"**.

3. Bake for about 20 minutes. Dish out immediately and enjoy warm.

Lemon Pepper Chicken

Preparation time: 5 minutes

Cooking Time: 20 minutes

Overall time: 25 minutes

Serves: 2 to 4 people

Recipe Ingredients:

- ❖ 1 tablespoon of lemon pepper
- ❖ 4 boneless skinless chicken breasts
- ❖ 1 teaspoon of table salt
- ❖ 1½ teaspoons of granulated garlic

Cooking Instructions:

1. Select the "Grill" button on the Ninja Foodi Smart XL Grill and regulate the time for 20 minutes at Medium.

2. Season the chicken breasts with salt, granulated garlic, and lemon pepper.

3. Place the chicken in the Ninja Foodi when it shows **"Add Food."** Grill for about 20 minutes, flipping halfway through cooking.

4. Dish out, plate and serve warm.

Chicken Broccoli

Preparation time: 5 minutes

Cooking Time: 20 minutes

Overall time: 25 minutes

Serves: 2 to 4 people

Recipe Ingredients:

- ❖ 1 tablespoon of olive oil
- ❖ 1 pound of boneless chicken breast (cut into bite-sized pieces)
- ❖ ½ pound of broccoli (cut into small florets)
- ❖ 1 tablespoon of soy sauce low sodium
- ❖ 2 teaspoons hot sauce
- ❖ Black pepper to taste
- ❖ ½ sliced onion
- ❖ ½ teaspoon of garlic powder
- ❖ 1 tablespoon of fresh minced ginger
- ❖ 1 teaspoon of sesame seed oil
- ❖ 2 teaspoons of rice vinegar
- ❖ Salt (to taste)

Cooking Instructions:

1. Select the "Grill" button on the Ninja Foodi Smart XL Grill and regulate the time for 20 minutes at Medium.

2. Combine the chicken breasts with onion and broccoli in a bowl. Toss in the remaining ingredients and mix thoroughly.

3. Place the chicken in the Ninja Foodi when it shows **"Add Food."** Grill for about 20 minutes, flipping halfway through cooking.

4. Dish out in a platter and top with lemon juice to serve. Enjoy!

Herb-Marinated Thighs

Preparation time: 5 minutes

Cooking Time: 18 minutes

Overall time: 23 minutes

Serves: 4 to 6 people

Recipe Ingredients:

- ❖ 2 teaspoons of garlic powder
- ❖ ¼ cup of olive oil
- ❖ 6 chicken thighs, (bone-in, skin-on)
- ❖ 2 teaspoons of lemon juice
- ❖ ½ teaspoon of dried sage
- ❖ 1 teaspoon of dried basil
- ❖ 1 teaspoon of spike seasoning
- ❖ ½ teaspoon of dried oregano
- ❖ ½ teaspoon of onion powder
- ❖ ¼ teaspoon of black pepper

Cooking Instructions:

1. Select the "Roast" button on the Ninja Foodi Smart XL Grill and regulate the time for 18 minutes.

2. Combine the chicken thighs with olive oil, onion powder, lemon juice, spike seasoning, garlic powder, oregano, basil, sage, and black pepper in a bowl.

3. Mix thoroughly and refrigerate to marinate for about 6 hours. Place the chicken thighs in the Ninja Foodi when it shows **"Add Food."**

4. Roast for about 18 minutes, flipping halfway through. Once done, dish out and serve warm.

Crispy Chicken and Potatoes

Preparation time: 5 minutes

Cooking Time: 15 minutes

Overall time: 20 minutes

Serves: 2 to 4 people

Recipe Ingredients:

- ❖ 1 teaspoon of olive oil
- ❖ 15 ounces of can drained potatoes
- ❖ 1 teaspoon of Lawry's seasoned salt
- ❖ 8 ounces of boneless, skinless, and cubed chicken breast,
- ❖ 3/8 cup of shredded cheddar cheese
- ❖ 1/8 teaspoon of black pepper
- ❖ ¼ teaspoon of paprika
- ❖ 4 slices of cooked bacon (cut into strips)

Cooking Instructions:

1. Select the "Broil" button on the Ninja Foodi Smart XL Grill and regulate the time for 20 minutes.

2. Toss the chicken and potato pieces with olive oil and spices. Place the chicken and potatoes in the Ninja Foodi when it shows **"Add Food".**

3. Top with bacon and cheese and start broiling, flipping halfway through.

4. Dish out in a platter and top with dried herbs to serve. Enjoy!

Crispy Chicken Thighs

Preparation time: 5 minutes

Cooking Time: 18 minutes

Overall time: 23 minutes

Serves: 2 to 4 people

Recipe Ingredients:

- ❖ 4 chicken thighs, (skin on, bone removed)
- ❖ Salt
- ❖ Garlic powder
- ❖ Black pepper (for garnishing)

Cooking Instructions:

1. Select the "Air Crisp" button on the Ninja Foodi Smart XL Grill and regulate the time for 18 minutes at 400°F.

2. Season the chicken with garlic powder and salt. Place the chicken in the Ninja Foodi when it shows **"Add Food."**

3. Air crisp for 18 minutes, flipping halfway through cooking.

4. Dish out in a platter and top with black pepper to serve.

5. Serve warm and enjoy.

Seafood Air Crisped Salmon

Preparation time: 5 minutes

Cooking Time: 8 minutes

Overall time: 13 minutes

Serves: 2 people

Recipe Ingredients:

- ❖ 2 salmon fillets
- ❖ 4 teaspoons of avocado oil
- ❖ 4 teaspoons of paprika
- ❖ Salt and coarse black pepper,
- ❖ Lemon wedges

Cooking Instructions:

1. Select the "Air Crisp" button on the Ninja Foodi Smart XL Grill and regulate the time for 8 minutes at 390ºF.

2. Rub the salmon fillets with salt, black pepper, avocado oil, and paprika.

3. Place the salmon fillets in the Ninja Foodi when it shows **"Add Food."** Air crisp for about 8 minutes, tossing the fillets halfway.

4. Dish out the fillets in a platter and serve warm.

5. Enjoy!

Broiled Tilapia

Preparation time: 5 minutes

Cooking Time: 8 minutes

Overall time: 13 minutes

Serves: 2 people

Recipe Ingredients:

- ❖ 1 pound of tilapia fillets old Bay seasoning
- ❖ Lemon pepper
- ❖ Salt
- ❖ Molly my butter
- ❖ Cooking oil spray

Cooking Instructions:

1. Select the "Broil" button on the Ninja Foodi Smart XL Grill and regulate the time for 8 minutes.

2. Rub the tilapia fillets with all the seasonings. Place the tilapia fillets in the Ninja Foodi when it shows **"Add Food"**.

3. Sprinkle with cooking oil spray and broil for about 8 minutes, tossing the fillets halfway.

4. Dish out the fillets in a platter, serve warm and enjoy.

Southern Catfish

Preparation time: 5 minutes

Cooking Time: 13 minutes

Overall time: 18 minutes

Serves: 2 to 4 people

Recipe Ingredients:

- ❖ 2 pounds catfish fillets
- ❖ 1 lemon
- ❖ 1 cup milk
- ❖ ½ cup yellow mustard

Cornmeal Seasoning Mix

- ❖ ½ cup of cornmeal
- ❖ 2 tablespoons of dried parsley flakes
- ❖ ¼ cup of all-purpose flour
- ❖ ½ teaspoon of kosher salt
- ❖ ¼ teaspoon of chili powder
- ❖ ¼ teaspoon of onion powder
- ❖ ¼ teaspoon of freshly ground black pepper
- ❖ ¼ teaspoon of garlic powder
- ❖ ¼ teaspoon of cayenne pepper

Cooking Instructions:

1. Select the "Air Crisp" button on the Ninja Foodi Smart XL Grill and regulate the time for 13 minutes at 400°F.

2. Combine the Catfish with milk and lemon juice and refrigerate for about 15 minutes.

3. Mix well the cornmeal seasoning ingredients in a bowl. Pat-dry the catfish fillets and rub with mustard.

4. Coat the catfish fillets with cornmeal mixture and transfer the fillets in the Ninja Foodi when it shows **"Add Food."**

5. Spray with cooking oil and air crisp for about 10 minutes, tossing the fillets halfway.

6. Serve the fillets in a platter and enjoy while warm.

Chili Lime Tilapia

Preparation time: 5 minutes

Cooking Time: 10 minutes

Overall time: 15 minutes

Serves: 2 people

Recipe Ingredients:

- ❖ 1 cup of panko crumbs
- ❖ 1 pound of tilapia fillets
- ❖ ½ cup of flour
- ❖ 1 tablespoon of chili powder
- ❖ Salt and black pepper
- ❖ 2 eggs
- ❖ 1 lime juiced

Cooking Instructions:

1. Select the "Grill" button on the Ninja Foodi Smart XL Grill and regulate the time for 10 minutes at Medium.

2. Combine the panko with salt, chili powder, and black pepper in a bowl.

3. Put the flour in one bowl and whisk an egg in another bowl. Then dredge the fillets in the flour and dip in the egg.

4. Coat with the panko mixture and place the fillets in the Ninja Foodi when it shows **"Add Food".** Grill for about 10 minutes, tossing the fillets halfway.

5. Dish out the fillets in a platter and drizzle with lime juice to serve. Enjoy!

Tuna Patties

Preparation time: 5 minutes

Cooking Time: 10 minutes

Overall time: 15 minutes

Serves: 4 people

Recipe Ingredients:

- ❖ 1½ tablespoons of almond flour
- ❖ 2 cans of tuna (packed in water)
- ❖ 1½ tablespoons of mayo
- ❖ 1 teaspoon of garlic powder
- ❖ Pinch of salt and pepper
- ❖ 1 teaspoon of dried dill
- ❖ ½ teaspoon of onion powder
- ❖ ½ lemon juiced

Cooking Instructions:

1. Select the "Grill" button on the Ninja Foodi Smart XL Grill and regulate the time for 10 minutes at Medium.

2. Combine all the tuna patties ingredients in a bowl and make equal-sized patties out of this mixture.

3. Place the tuna patties in the Ninja Foodi when it shows **"Add Food".**

4. Grill for about 10 minutes, tossing the patties halfway through cooking.

5. Serve the fillets in a platter and enjoy warm.

Ingredients Catfish

Preparation time: 5 minutes

Cooking Time: 12 minutes

Overall time: 17 minutes

Serves: 2 to 4 people

Recipe Ingredients:

- ❖ ¼ cup of louisiana fish seasoning
- ❖ 1 tablespoon of chopped parsley,
- ❖ 4 catfish fillets
- ❖ 1 tablespoon of olive oil

Cooking Instructions:

1. Select the "Grill" button on the Ninja Foodi Smart XL Grill and regulate the time for 12 minutes at Medium.

2. Combine the catfish fillets with Louisiana fish seasoning in a bowl and stir.

3. Place the fillets in the Ninja Foodi when it shows **"Add Food"** and spray with olive oil. Grill for about 10 minutes, tossing the patties halfway through.

4. Dish out the fillets in a platter and garnish with parsley.

5. Serve immediately and enjoy.

Breaded Shrimp

Preparation time: 5 minutes

Cooking Time: 16 minutes

Overall time: 21 minutes

Serves: 2 to 4 people

Recipe Ingredients:

- ❖ 2 eggs
- ❖ 1 pound of shrimp, peeled and deveined
- ❖ ½ cup of panko breadcrumbs
- ❖ 1 teaspoon of ginger
- ❖ 1 teaspoon of garlic powder
- ❖ ½ cup of peeled and diced onion
- ❖ 1 teaspoon of black pepper

Cooking Instructions:

1. Select the "Air Crisp" button on the Ninja Foodi Smart XL Grill and regulate the time for 16 minutes at 350°F.

2. Combine panko, spices, and onions in one bowl, and whisk eggs in another bowl.

3. Dip the shrimp in the whisked eggs and then dredge in the panko mixture.

4. Place the shrimp in the Ninja Foodi when it shows **"Add Food."** Then grill for about 16 minutes, tossing the patties halfway through cooking.

5. Dish out the fillets in a platter and serve warm. Enjoy your meal!

MEAT RECIPES

Asparagus Steak Tips

Preparation time: 5 minutes

Cooking Time: 25 minutes

Overall time: 30 minutes

Serves: 2 people

Recipe Ingredients:

❖ 1 pound of steak cubes
❖ 1 teaspoon of olive oil
❖ ½ teaspoon of salt
❖ ½ teaspoon of dried garlic powder
❖ 1/8 teaspoon of cayenne pepper
❖ ½ teaspoon of freshly ground black pepper,
❖ ½ teaspoon of dried onion powder air-fryer asparagus
❖ ¼ teaspoon of salt
❖ 1 pound of asparagus, tough ends trimmed
❖ ½ teaspoon of olive oil

Cooking Instructions:

1. Press the "Grill" button on the Ninja Foodi Smart XL, Grill and regulate the time for 10 minutes at Medium.

2. Combine garlic powder, onion powder, cayenne pepper, salt, and black pepper in a bowl.

3. Place the steak cubes in a Ziploc bag and add garlic powder mixture.

4. Shake the bag well and transfer the steak cubes in the Ninja Foodi when it shows **"Add Food."**

5. Grill for 10 minutes, tossing the steaks halfway. After that, season the asparagus with salt and drizzle with olive oil.

6. Add the asparagus into the Ninja Foodi and grill for about 5 minutes.

7. Dish out in a platter and serve warm.

Korean BBQ Beef

Preparation time: 5 minutes

Cooking Time: 15 minutes

Overall time: 20 minutes

Serves: 2 people

Recipe Ingredients:

For The Meat:

- ❖ 1 pound of flank steak
- ❖ Coconut oil spray
- ❖ ¼ cup of corn starch

For The Sauce:

- ❖ ½ cup of brown sugar
- ❖ ½ cup of soy sauce
- ❖ 2 tablespoons of pompeian white wine vinegar
- ❖ 1 tablespoon of hot chili sauce
- ❖ ½ teaspoon of sesame seeds
- ❖ 1 teaspoon of water
- ❖ 1 clove of crushed garlic,
- ❖ 1 teaspoon of ground ginger
- ❖ 1 teaspoon of cornstarch

Cooking Instructions:

1. Select the "Grill" button on the Ninja Foodi Smart XL Grill and regulate the time for 10 minutes at Medium.

2. Grease the grill with the coconut oil spray. Then dredge the steaks in the cornstarch and transfer into the Ninja Foodi when it shows "Add Food."

3. Combine the rest of the ingredients for the sauce in a pan except cornstarch and water.

4. Whisk cornstarch with water in a bowl and add to the sauce.

5. Cook on medium-low heat until it thickens, and pour the sauce over the steaks to serve.

6. Delicious!

Steak and Mushrooms

Preparation time: 1 hr. 5 minutes

Cooking Time: 10 minutes

Overall time: 1 hr. 15 minutes

Serves: 2 to 4 people

Recipe Ingredients:

- ❖ 1 pound of beef sirloin steak (cubed into 1-inch pieces)
- ❖ ¼ cup of worcestershire sauce
- ❖ 8 ounces of sliced mushrooms
- ❖ 1 tablespoon of olive oil
- ❖ 1 teaspoon of parsley flakes
- ❖ 1 teaspoon of paprika
- ❖ 1 teaspoon of crushed chili flakes,

Cooking Instructions:

1. Select the "Air Crisp" button on the Ninja Foodi Smart XL Grill and regulate the time for 10 minutes at 400°F.

2. Combine the steak with olive oil, parsley, mushrooms, chili flakes, paprika, and Worcestershire sauce in a bowl.

3. Cover the bowl and marinate the steaks for about 3 hours in the refrigerator.

4. Place the steaks and mushrooms in the Ninja Foodi when it shows **"Add Food."** Air crisp for about 10 minutes, tossing well in the halfway.

5. Dish out in a platter and serve warm.

Herb Crusted Chops

Preparation time: 5 minutes

Cooking Time: 12 minutes

Overall time: 17 minutes

Serves: 2 people

Recipe Ingredients:

- ❖ 1 teaspoon of olive oil
- ❖ 1 pound of pork loin chops (bone-in)
- ❖ 1 tablespoon of herb and garlic seasoning

Cooking Instructions:

1. Select the "Air Crisp" button on the Ninja Foodi Smart XL Grill and regulate the time for 12 minutes at 350°F.

2. Combine the steak with olive oil and seasoning mixture in a bowl. Then place the steaks in the Ninja Foodi when it shows **"Add Food."**

3. Air crisp for about 12 minutes, flipping halfway through cooking.

4. Serve immediately and enjoy while warm.

Memphis-Style Pork Ribs

Preparation time: 5 minutes

Cooking Time: 20 minutes

Overall time: 25 minutes

Serves: 6 people

Recipe Ingredients:
- 1 tablespoon of sweet paprika
- 1 teaspoon of onion powder
- ½ teaspoon of mustard powder
- 2¼ pounds of pork spareribs
- 1 tablespoon kosher salt
- 1 tablespoon of dark brown sugar
- 1 teaspoon of garlic powder

- 1 teaspoon of poultry seasoning
- ½ teaspoon of freshly ground black pepper

Cooking instructions:

1. Select the "Grill" button on the Ninja Foodi Smart XL Grill and regulate the time for 35 minutes at Medium.

2. Combine poultry seasoning, salt, onion powder, sugar, paprika, pepper, mustard powder, and garlic powder in a bowl.

3. Dredge the pork ribs in the poultry seasoning mixture and rub well.

4. Place the pork ribs in the Ninja Foodi when it shows **"Add Food."** Grill for about 20 minutes, flipping halfway through.

5. Dish out in a plate and serve warm. Enjoy!

Crispy Pork Belly

Preparation time: 1 hr. 5 minutes

Cooking Time: 20 minutes

Overall time: 1 hr. 25 minutes

Serves: 4 people

Recipe Ingredients:

- ❖ ½ cup of coconut aminos
- ❖ 2 packages of pork belly (diced into 1-inch cubes)
- ❖ ½ cup of coconut vinegar
- ❖ ¼ teaspoon of fish sauce Salt, to taste

* ❖ ¼ cup of sriracha coconut oil spray

Cooking Instructions:

1. Select "Air Crisp" button on the Ninja Foodi Smart XL Grill and regulate the time for 20 minutes at Medium.

2. Combine pork belly with fish sauce, coconut vinegar, aminos, and Sriracha in a Ziploc bag.

3. Shake the Ziploc bag to coat the pork belly well and preserve for about 2 hours.

4. Place the pork cubes in the Ninja Foodi when it shows **"Add Food."** After that, pour oil and salt on the pork and start cooking.

5. Flip the sides of the pork after 10 minutes and season this side with salt and oil.

6. Air crisp for the remaining 10 minutes and dish out to serve warm.

Beef Satay

Preparation time: 35 minutes

Cooking Time: 15 minutes

Overall time: 50 minutes

Serves: 2 people

Recipe Ingredients:

* ❖ 2 tablespoons of olive oil
* ❖ 1 pound of beef flank steak (sliced into long strips)
* ❖ 1 tablespoon of fish sauce
* ❖ 1 tablespoon of minced ginger

- ❖ 1 tablespoon of sugar
- ❖ 1 teaspoon of ground coriander
- ❖ ¼ cup of peanuts of roasted and chopped
- ❖ 1 tablespoon of soy sauce
- ❖ 1 tablespoon of minced garlic,
- ❖ 1 teaspoon of sriracha sauce
- ❖ ½ cup of chopped and divided cilantro

Cooking Instructions:

1. Select "Grill" button on the Ninja Foodi Smart XL Grill and regulate the time for 15 minutes at Medium.

2. Merge fish sauce with soy sauce, ginger, garlic, coriander, Sriracha, sugar, and ¼ cup cilantro in a bowl.

3. Dredge the beef strips in the fish sauce mixture and preserve for about 30 minutes.

4. Place the beef strips in the Ninja Foodi when it shows **"Add Food"** and drizzle with olive oil. Then grill for 15 minutes, flipping in a middle way.

5. Garnished with cilantro and roasted peanuts. Serve and enjoy.

Sides Lemon Tofu

Preparation time: 30 minutes

Cooking Time: 20 minutes

Overall time: 50 minutes

Serves: 2 people

Recipe Ingredients:

- ❖ 1 pound of extra-firm tofu (drained, pressed, and cubed)
- ❖ 1 tablespoon of tamari

- ❖ 1 tablespoon of arrowroot powder

For the Sauce:

- ❖ ½ cup of water
- ❖ 1/3 cup of lemon juice
- ❖ 1 teaspoon of lemon zest
- ❖ 2 teaspoons of arrowroot powder
- ❖ 2 tablespoons of organic sugar

Cooking Instructions:

1. Select "Grill" button on the Ninja Foodi Smart XL Grill and regulate the time for 15 minutes.

2. Place the tofu, arrowroot powder, and tamari in a Ziploc bag.

3. Seal the Ziploc bag, shake it thoroughly, and preserve for about 30 minutes. Put the tofu in the Ninja Foodi when it shows **"Add Food."**

4. Stir the tofu halfway through grilling and dish out in a plate when completely grilled.

5. Put all the ingredients for the sauce in a skillet and cook for about 5 minutes on medium-low heat.

6. Place the tofu in the sauce and serve. Enjoy!

Spicy Cauliflower

Preparation time: 5 minutes

Cooking Time: 20 minutes

Overall time: 25 minutes

Serves: 2 to 4 people

Recipe Ingredients:

- ❖ 3/4 cup of thinly sliced white onion

- ❖ 1 head of cauliflower (cut into florets)
- ❖ 5 finely sliced garlic cloves
- ❖ 1 tablespoon of rice vinegar
- ❖ 1 tablespoon of sriracha
- ❖ 1½ tablespoons of tamari
- ❖ ½ teaspoon of coconut sugar
- ❖ 2 scallions (for garnishing)

Cooking Instructions:

1. Select the "Grill" button on the Ninja Foodi Smart XL Grill and regulate the time for 10 minutes.

2. Put the cauliflowers in the Ninja Foodi when it shows **"Add Food."** Add the onions and garlic after 10 minutes and grill for 5 minutes.

3. Combine sugar, soy sauce, salt, pepper, rice vinegar, and Sriracha in a bowl.

4. Then pour the sugar mixture over the cauliflower and grill for another 5 minutes.

5. Dish out in a plate when completely grilled and garnish with scallions.

6. Serve immediately and enjoy.

Crispy Artichoke Fries

Preparation time: 5 minutes

Cooking Time: 13 minutes

Overall time: 18 minutes

Serves: 2 to 4 people

Recipe Ingredients:

- 14 ounces can of artichoke hearts (quartered)

For the wet mix:

- 1 cup of almond milk
- 1 cup of all-purpose flour
- ½ teaspoon of garlic powder
- ¼ teaspoon of black pepper, or to taste
- ¾ teaspoon of salt

For the dry mix:

- ½ teaspoon of paprika
- 1½ cups of panko bread crumbs
- ¼ teaspoon of salt

Cooking Instructions:

1. Select the "Air Crisp" button on the Ninja Foodi Smart XL Grill and regulate the temperature to 375°F for 13 minutes.

2. Fold all the dry ingredients in one bowl and wet ingredients in another bowl.

3. Dip the artichokes in the wet mixture and then dredge in the dry mixture.

4. Put the artichokes in the Ninja Foodi when it shows **"Add Food."**

5. Dish out the artichokes in a bowl to serve when completely air crisped.

Corn Fritters

Preparation time: 5 minutes

Cooking Time: 5 minutes

Overall time: 10 minutes

Serves: 2 to 4 people

Recipe Ingredients:

- ❖ 1/3 cup of finely ground cornmeal
- ❖ 2 cups of frozen corn kernels
- ❖ 1/3 cup of flour
- ❖ ¼ teaspoon of black pepper
- ❖ ½ teaspoon of baking powder
- ❖ Garlic powder (to taste)
- ❖ 2 tablespoons of green chiles
- ❖ Juices vegetable oil (for frying)
- ❖ ½ teaspoon of salt
- ❖ Onion powder (to taste)
- ❖ ¼ teaspoon of paprika
- ❖ ¼ cup of chopped Italian parsley

For The Tangy Dipping Sauce:
- ❖ 4 teaspoons of dijon mustard
- ❖ 4 tablespoons of vegan mayonnaise
- ❖ 2 teaspoons of grainy mustard

Cooking Instructions:

1. Select the "Air Crisp" button on the Ninja Foodi Smart XL Grill and regulate the temperature to 375ºF for 5 minutes.

2. Combine flour, baking powder, seasonings, parsley, and cornmeal in a bowl.

3. Put 1 cup corn with salt, 3 tablespoons almond milk and pepper in a food processor and process until smooth.

4. Fold the corn mixture into the flour mixture until thoroughly combined.

5. Stir in the remaining corn kernels and spread this mixture in a pan. Then put the pan in the Ninja Foodi when it shows **"Add Food."**

6. Slice and dish out the corn fritters in a bowl. Whisk all the tangy dipping sauce ingredients in a bowl and serve with corn fritters.

7. Enjoy!

Tofu Italian Style

Preparation time: 5 minutes

Cooking Time: 6 minutes

Overall time: 11 minutes

Serves: 2 to 4 people

Recipe Ingredients:

- ❖ 1 tablespoon of tamari
- ❖ 8 ounces of extra-firm tofu (pressed and cubed)
- ❖ 1 tablespoon of aquafaba
- ❖ ½ teaspoon of dried basil
- ❖ ¼ teaspoon of granulated onion
- ❖ ½ teaspoon of dried oregano
- ❖ ½ teaspoon of granulated garlic
- ❖ Black pepper to taste

Cooking Instructions:

1. Select the "Air Crisp" button on the Ninja Foodi Smart XL Grill and regulate the temperature to 400ºF for 6 minutes.
2. Mix-up the tofu with the remaining ingredients in a bowl and preserve for 20 minutes.
3. Put the tofu in the Ninja Foodi when it shows "Add Food." Dish out the tofu when completely cooked.
4. Serve warm and enjoy.

Grilled Vegetables

Preparation time: 10 minutes

Cooking Time: 10 minutes

Overall time: 20 minutes

Serves: 2 to 3 people

Recipe Ingredients:

- ❖ 1 pound of trimmed asparagus
- ❖ 1½ tablespoons of olive oil
- ❖ ½ pound of cherry tomatoes stemmed
- ❖ 1 corn ear (cut crosswise into 4 pieces)
- ❖ Salt and black pepper, to taste
- ❖ 4 ounces of halved cremini mushrooms,
- ❖ 1 zucchini, quartered lengthwise

For the Basil Garlic Sauce:

- ❖ 1¼ tablespoons red wine vinegar
- ❖ ¼ cup olive oil
- ❖ ½ teaspoon Dijon mustard
- ❖ ¼ cup fresh basil leaves,
- ❖ packed Salt and black pepper, to taste
- ❖ 1 garlic clove, chopped
- ❖ 1½ tablespoons fresh parsley leaves, packed

Cooking Instructions:

1. Select the "Grill" button on the Ninja Foodi Smart XL Grill and regulate the time for 20 minutes.

2. Put all the basil garlic sauce ingredients in a food processor and process until smooth.

3. Season the asparagus, mushrooms, tomatoes, zucchini, and corn with salt and black pepper, and drizzle with olive oil.

4. Transfer the vegetables in the Ninja Foodi when it shows **"Add Food."**

5. Dish out the tomatoes, mushrooms, and asparagus after 5 minutes and zucchini and corn after 10 minutes. Serve warm with basil garlic sauce. Enjoy!

DESSERTS RECIPES

Grilled Pineapple Sundaes

Preparation time: 10 minutes

Cooking Time: 6 minutes

Overall time: 16 minutes

Serves: 2 to 4 people

Recipe Ingredients:

- ❖ 4 scoops of vanilla ice cream
- ❖ 2 tablespoons of toasted and shredded sweetened coconut
- ❖ 4 slices of pineapple
- ❖ Dulce de leche (for drizzling)

Cooking Instructions:

1. Select the "Grill" button on the Ninja Foodi Smart XL Grill and regulate the time for 4 minutes.

2. Put the pineapple slices in the Ninja Foodi when it shows **"Add Food."**

3. Flip the pineapple slices after 2 minutes. When completely grilled, dish out on a plate.

4. Put the vanilla ice cream scoops on the grilled pineapple slices.

5. Drizzle Dulce de leche and sprinkle shredded coconut over the pineapples.

6. Serve immediately and enjoy!

S'mores Roll-Up

Preparation time: 10 minutes

Cooking Time: 7 ½ minutes

Overall time: 17 ½ minutes

Serves: 2 people

Recipe Ingredients:

- ❖ 2 cups mini marshmallows
- ❖ 4 graham crackers
- ❖ 2 flour tortillas
- ❖ 2 cups chocolate chips

Cooking Instructions:

1. Select the "Grill" button on the Ninja Foodi Smart XL Grill and regulate the time for 5 minutes.

2. Divide the chocolate chips, graham crackers, and marshmallows on the tortillas.

3. Wrap up the tortilla tightly and place it inside the Ninja Foodi when it shows **"Add Food."**

4. Flip the tortillas after 2½ minutes and dish out in a plate when completely grilled.

5. Serve and enjoy!

Grilled Donut Ice Cream Sandwich

Preparation time: 10 minutes

Cooking Time: 3 minutes

Overall time: 13 minutes

Serves: 2 to 4 people

Recipe Ingredients:

- ❖ 8 scoops of vanilla ice cream
- ❖ 4 glazed donuts, (cut in half)
- ❖ Chocolate syrup (for drizzling)
- ❖ 4 cherries maraschino
- ❖ 1 cup of whipped cream

Cooking Instructions:

1. Select the "Grill" button on the Ninja Foodi Smart XL Grill and regulate the time for 3 minutes.

2. Place the donut halves, glazed side down, inside the Ninja Foodi when it shows **"Add Food."**

3. Dish out in a platter and fill each donut sandwich with vanilla ice cream.

4. Drizzle the chocolate syrup on the donuts and top with whipped cream and cherry.

5. Plate, serve and enjoy.

Grilled Fruit Skewers

Preparation time: 10 minutes

Cooking Time: 12 minutes

Overall time: 22 minutes

Serves: 5 to 8 people

Recipe Ingredients:

- ❖ 1½ pints of sliced strawberries
- ❖ 8 sliced peaches
- ❖ 1½ cups of pineapples (cut into large cubes)
- ❖ 3 tablespoons of olive oil (for drizzling)
- ❖ 3 tablespoons of honey (for drizzling)
- ❖ 10 skewers soaked in water
- ❖ 20 minutes salt (to taste)

Cooking Instructions:

1. Select the "Grill" button on the Ninja Foodi Smart XL Grill and adjust the time for 12 minutes at Medium.

2. Put the strawberries, pineapples, and peaches on the skewers. Season with salt and drizzle with olive oil.

3. Place the skewers inside the Ninja Foodi when it shows **"Add Food."**

4. Allow to grill, turning twice in between.Top the grilled fruits with honey.

5. Serve immediately and enjoy.

Chocolate Marshmallow Banana

Preparation time: 10 minutes

Cooking Time: 5 minutes

Overall time: 15 minutes

Serves: 2 people

Recipe Ingredients:

- ❖ 1 cup of chocolate chips
- ❖ 2 peeled bananas
- ❖ 1 cup of mini marshmallows

Cooking Directions:

1. Select the "Grill" button on the Ninja Foodi Smart XL Grill and regulate the time for 5 minutes.

2. Put the banana on a foil paper and slice it lengthwise, leaving the ends.

3. Put the chocolate chips and marshmallows inside the bananas and tightly wrap the foil.

4. Place the filled bananas inside the Ninja Foodi when it shows "Add Food."

5. Dish out in a platter and unwrap to serve and enjoy.

Bloomin' Grilled Apples

Preparation time: 10 minutes

Cooking Time: 30 minutes

Overall time: 40 minutes

Serves: 4 people

Recipe Ingredients:

- ❖ 4 scoops of vanilla ice cream
- ❖ 8 tablespoons of maple cream caramel sauce (divided)
- ❖ 4 small baking apples
- ❖ 12 teaspoons of chopped pecans (divided)

Cooking Instructions:

1. Select the "Grill" button on the Ninja Foodi Smart XL Grill and regulate the time for 30 minutes.

2. Chop off the upper part of the apples and scoop the core out of the apples.

3. Cut the apple around the center and insert narrow cuts surrounding the apple.

4. Put the pecans and maple cream caramel sauce in the center of the apple.

5. Wrap the foil around the apple and put the apple inside the Ninja Foodi when it shows **"Add Food."**

6. Dish out in a platter and top with vanilla ice cream scoop.

7. Serve and enjoy.

Acknowledgement

In preparing the "Ninja Foodi Smart XL Grill Cookbook", I sincerely wish to acknowledge my indebtedness to my husband for his support and the wholehearted cooperation and vast experience of my two colleagues - Mrs. Alexandra Bedria, and Mrs. Rebecca Pace.

Michelle Lively

CPSIA information can be obtained
at www.ICGtesting.com
Printed in the USA
BVHW052329040521
606420BV00002B/713